first edition 2009
wallymeets publishing
wallymeets.com

wally meets picasso

printed in the united states

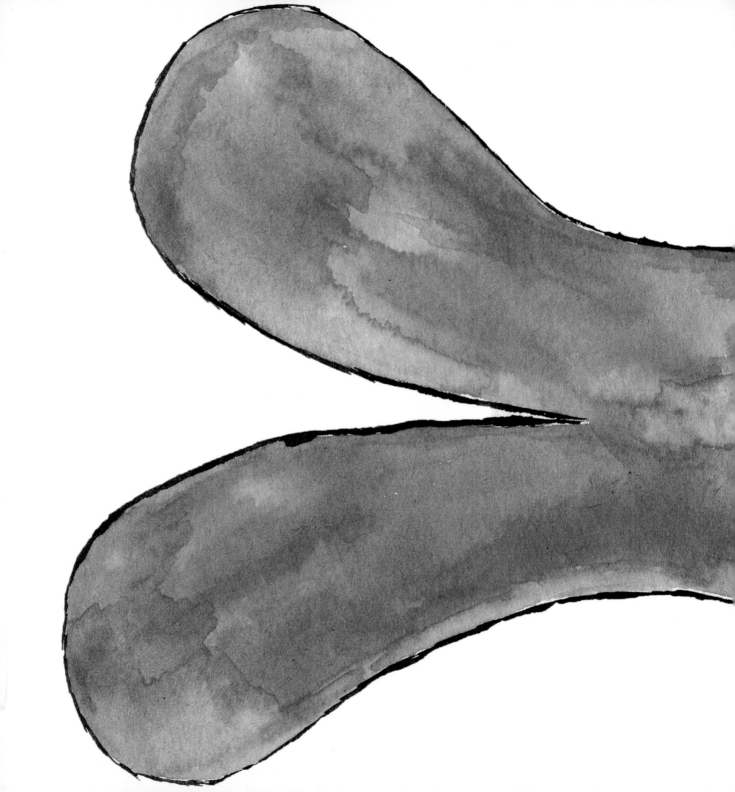

this is wally
wally is a baby whale
he is almost four years old

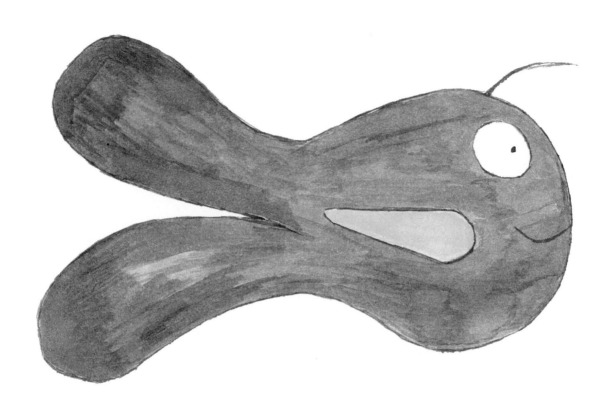

today wally is drawing a fish

wally shows the drawing to his mama

"what a pretty drawing wally," says wally's mama

wally wants to make another drawing

but there is no more paint

"mama, mama, there is no more paint!" says wally

wally and his mama swim to the

paint store to buy new paint

in the store window wally sees a painting

"what a beautiful painting," says wally and runs into the store

"wait!" says wally's mama, but wally is already gone

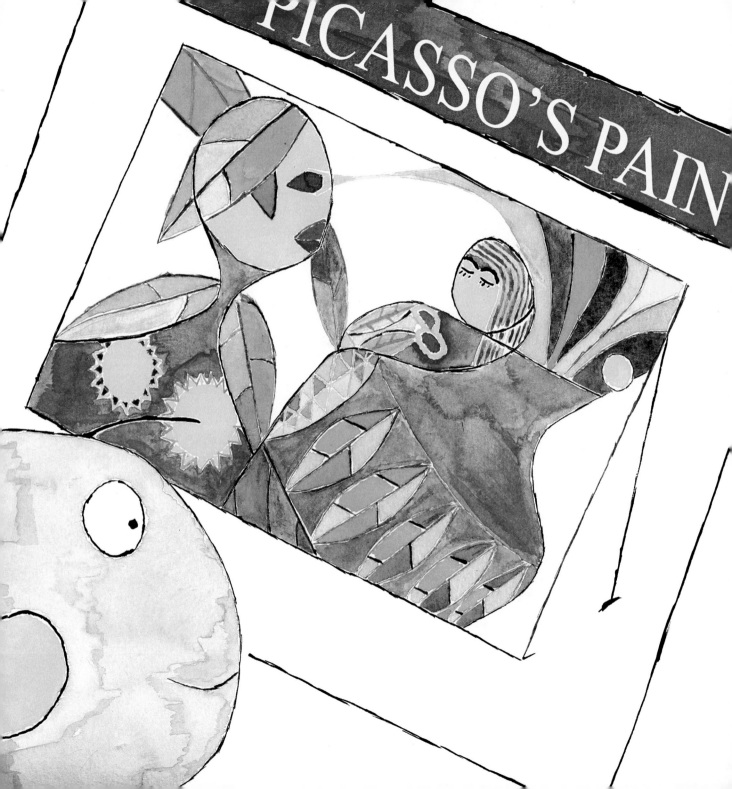

"hello, my name is wally"

"hello wally, my name is picasso"

"do you make these wonderful drawings?" asks wally

"yes wally, i'm a painter," explains picasso

"can you also paint a whale?" asks wally

"if you sit still i will make a painting of you," says picasso

wally sits ever so still as picasso paints his picture

but when wally sees the paint- ing he is shocked...

"i don't look like that at all!"
shouts wally panicky

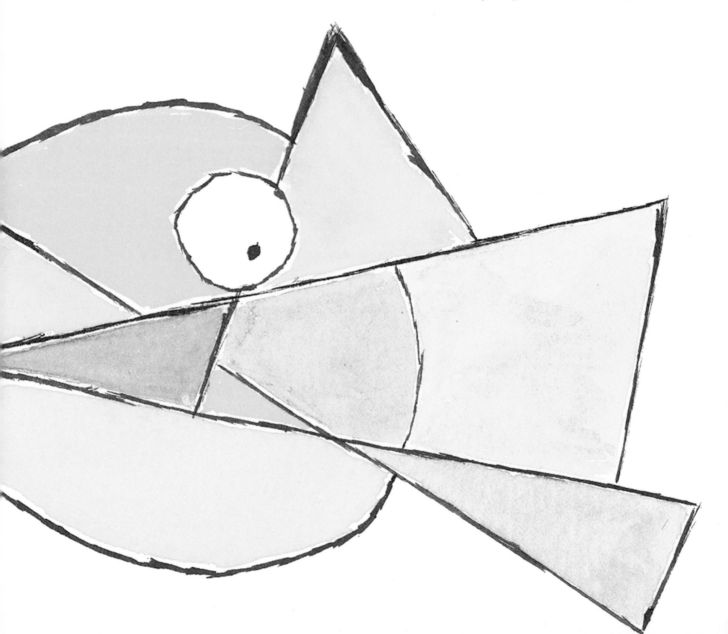

"wally, this is my imagination, like when you have a fantasy or dream," picasso explains

wally understands "so when i imagine that you are a picasso fish, then i can draw you like a fish?"

"yes wally, that is correct," says picasso

"can i draw you now picasso?"
asks wally

wally draws picasso

picasso looks at wally's drawing
and says:

"well done wally
never stop dreaming"

wally is very happy

wally smiles and says "i want to be a painter so i can dream every day--"

"--thank you picasso"

Isgar Bos started writing children books to compensate for the panic and fear around him.

As an airport engineer he traveled around the world and he realized that children are everywhere he same.

It is society that makes them different. Isgar wants to share the positive and innocent world with children everywhere.

Made in the USA
San Bernardino, CA
27 June 2016